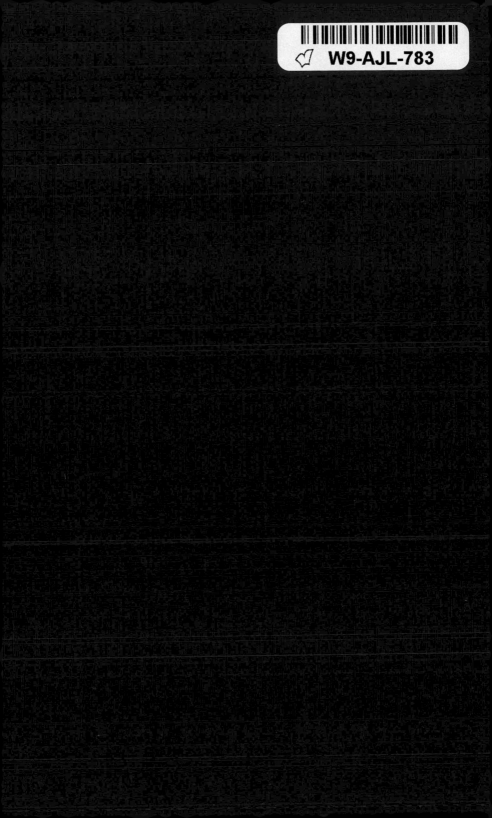

THE
MILK
HOURS

THE
MILK
HOURS

POEMS BY JOHN JAMES

MAX RITVO POETRY PRIZE | SELECTED BY HENRI COLE

MILKWEED EDITIONS

Published 2019 by Milkweed Editions
Printed in Canada
Cover design by Mary Austin Speaker
Cover art is in the public domain
Author photo by Gina Collecchia
19 20 21 22 23 5 4 3 2 1
First Edition

Milkweed Editions, an independent nonprofit publisher, gratefully acknowledges
sustaining support from the Ballard Spahr Foundation; the Jerome Foundation; the
McKnight Foundation; the National Endowment for the Arts; the Target Foundation; and
other generous contributions from foundations, corporations, and individuals. Also, this
activity is made possible by the voters of Minnesota through a Minnesota State Arts Board
Operating Support grant, thanks to a legislative appropriation from the arts and cultural
heritage fund. For a full listing of Milkweed Editions supporters, please visit milkweed.org.

Library of Congress Cataloging-in-Publication Data

Names: James, John (Poet), author.
Title: The milk hours : poems / John James.
Description: First edition. | Minneapolis, Minnesota : Milkweed
Editions, 2019. | Includes bibliographical references.
Identifiers: LCCN 2019001447 (print) | LCCN 2019003544 (ebook)
| ISBN 9781571317247 (ebook) | ISBN 9781571315083 (pbk. : alk.
paper) Classification: LCC PS3610.A4296 (ebook) | LCC PS3610.
A4296 A6 2019 (print) |
  DDC 811/.6--dc23
LC record available at https://lccn.loc.gov/2019001447

Milkweed Editions is committed to ecological stewardship. We strive to align our book
production practices with this principle, and to reduce the impact of our operations in
the environment. We are a member of the Green Press Initiative, a nonprofit coalition
of publishers, manufacturers, and authors working to protect the world's endangered
forests and conserve natural resources. *The Milk Hours* was printed on acid-free 100%
postconsumer-waste paper by Friesens Corporation.

Contents

THE
MILK
HOURS

The Milk Hours

for J.E.J., 1962–1993
and C.S.M.J., 2013–

We lived overlooking the walls overlooking the cemetery.
The cemetery is where my father remains. We walked
in the garden for what seemed like an hour but in reality must
have been days. *Cattail, heartseed*—these words mean nothing to me.
The room opens up into white and more white, sun outside
between steeples. I remember, now, the milk hours, leaning
over my daughter's crib, dropping her ten, twelve pounds
into the limp arms of her mother. The suckling sound as I crashed
into sleep. My daughter, my father—*his son.* The wet grass
dew-speckled above him. His face grows vague and then vaguer.
From our porch I watch snow fall on bare firs. Why does it
matter now—what gun, what type. Bluesmoke rises. The chopped
copses glisten. Snowmelt smoothes the stone cuts of his name.

§

History (n.)

Viewed from space, the Chilean volcano blooms.

I cannot see it. It's a problem of scale. *History*—the branch

of knowledge dealing with past events; a continuous,

systematic narrative of; aggregate deeds; acts, ideas, events

that will shape the course of the future; immediate

but significant happenings; finished, done with—"he's history."

—

Calbuco: men shoveling ash from the street.

Third time in a week. And counting.

Infinite antithesis. Eleven

miles of ash in the air. What to call it—

just "ash." They flee to Ensenada.

—

The power of motives does not proceed directly from the will—

a changed form of knowledge. Wind pushing

clouds toward Argentina. *Knowledge is merely involved.*

Ash falls, it is falling, it has fallen. *Will fall.* Already flights

cancelled in Buenos Aires. I want to call it "snow"—

what settles on the luma trees, their fruit black, purplish black,

soot-speckled, hermaphroditic—*if this book is unintelligible*

and hard on the ears—the oblong ovals of its leaves.

Amos, fragrant. Family name *Myrtus*. The wood is extremely hard.

—

Ash falling on the concrete, falling on cars, ash

on the windshields, windows, yards. *They have lost*

all sense of direction. They might as well be deep

in a forest or down in a well. They do not comprehend

the fundamental principles. They have nothing in their heads.

—

The dream kept

      urging me on to do

what I was doing—

      to make music—

since philosophy,

      in my view, is

            the greatest music.

—

      History—from the Greek *historía,* learning or knowing by inquiry. *Historein* (v.) to ask. *The asking is not idle.* From the French *histoire,* story. *Hístor* (Gk.) one who sees. *It is just a matter of what we are looking for.*

Metamorphoses

what was it this
morning : you said

redgrass glistens
in surf : the pine

board fence collapsed
along the line : after

the storm a kestrel
in headwind : sand

accumulates on your
feet : puckered seal

skin : the salt-washed
flesh : wreckage towing

upshore : when the
gulls came out I saw

them circling in air :
saw them pecking

seals' eyes from
torn skin : a boy

downstrand rolling
in dunes : I could see

the stomach's red
wall : the small hairs

on its flippers : blubber
wrenched by shark

bite from the belly's
swell : later seen

from a dune : black
water : fish spit

pooling : mouth open
enough to see teeth

trailing in sand : his lips
limp : there in

the storm's wake
I wanted something

to say : the ocean
scraped his insides clean

April, Andromeda

I am in this world, not self, not seed, not stamen-dusted

pistil flicking in the wind—the eye sees past its limitations.

Crushed petals in the dirt, I'm courting a horse with an apple,

watching its white tail swish along the fence. Somewhere,

the galaxy spins. I smile at the cloudless sky.

—

Continuum of frequencies, Ptolemy's

Almagest, the star charts called it *Little Cloud*—

chained constellations in *The Book*

of Fixed Stars. Nova for *new*, cut fish

for *never*. A heart held back for the knife.

—

The opening of large
tracts by the ice-
cutters commonly causes
a pond to break
up earlier; for the water
agitated by the wind
even in cold weather
wears away
the surrounding ice.

—

This morning I walked past
rows of jeweled honeysuckle
twining through the square
links in an aluminum fence.
They glistened in the sun,
as they always do. You
could say their vines shuddered.

—

Photographed by Isaac

Roberts, 1887, again

in 1899, the galaxy, the ruler

of man, the pearling

spiral takes its name from

the area of sky in which it appears.

Sussex, England, retrograde motion.

The daughter chained to a rock.

—

We forget rapidly what should be forgotten. The universal

sense of fables and anecdotes is marked by our tendency to forget

name and date and geography. "How in the right are children

to forget name and date and place."

—

Pained loveliness—the sonnet
sweet fetter'd. Morning, still, couched
in narrative—carrots taken
from my palm. Horse's muzzle,
its silken touch, teeth against the skin.
The eye sees the mind sees
crushed petals in the pestle.
All parts are binding.

—

Constellations—huge
man wearing a crown,
upside down with respect
to the eclipse. The smaller
figure next to him sitting
on a chair. A whale
somewhere beneath it.

—

By ear industrious—attention

met—misers of sound

and syllable. See kale, see

rows of collard stalks—think

Cassiopeia. Think arrogant

and vain. Greek models, sea

monster Cetus, the errant study of.

—

I shall ere long paint to you—as one can without

canvas—the true form of the whale—

my parts are all binding—

as he actually appears to the eye—

I wonder, now, how Ovid did it—*I pass that matter by.*

Poem for the Nation, 2016

When it's a weapon, when it flies,
the flag is a striped
        idea flapping on a pole. It makes a fine cape,
my daughter says. She wears it on the Fourth.

I say the pledge but never know
if I mean it or I don't. The alders bleed,
        the shot trees on the Capitol lawn
bend in the wind.
                        Heat collects
in the quarried stone
                of white buildings. "This is what
an ailing empire looks like," you say.

        I agree, watching mallards
spin on the Potomac. They paddle

on the surface
        of the reflecting pool, webbed feet
beating in assembly,
        one duck, then another, gathering on the grass

before they take flight.
        In grade school, hands on our hearts,
we sang the anthem, words not a one of us

        understood: the blasting, bombardments,
things I'd never heard or seen.

                        In the cut grass you kiss me.
I take your hand to my lips. We watch

the flags at half-mast parade around
          a white tower.
Helicopters hum,

          our daughter takes a grape in her hand.
You cut it in half, tell her not to choke.

          I gulp wine from a cup, litter
in the president's yard.
          All we ever needed
was a start.

Klee's Painting

This is how one pictures the angel of history.

—*Walter Benjamin, "On the Concept of History"*

It's not bad to have a body, chicken plucking

shells from the dirt, seals at the zoo

falling backward, swallowing a herring,

shuddering in the late autumn heat.

The keyboard of a piano divided into many notes.

The world thickens with its texture. *The lizard's eye*

flickered once more. Sometimes, staring back,

I fear its relevance, *Angelus Novus,* print

transferred to oil, ruin upon stumbling ruin. A single

chain of events. Little pile of scribbles.

This is the storm we call progress. Sugar maples,

the broadness of their leaves. Little silver bell,

open mouth of blossoms. So many things

      shiver in the cold. Name *kudzu*, genus *Pueraria*,

in the pea family. Chokes out native vegetation

      via heavy shading.

Used in the South to feed goats.

        §

I sit gossiping in the early

        candle-light of old age casting

backward glances over traveled roads. A perfect catastrophe

set into lines. *A varied*

        jaunt of years.

§

Leipzig, 1920s, a Jewish university student.

Boy with a disposition fragile as his breathing, born

to an assimilated upper-class family in the last

decade of the century before his own. Bankers

and antique traders. Factory owners. Grandfather

a successful chemist who fought in the army

of the Kaiser, returned home with a box

of medals on his chest. The body, no, it's not bad.

I am gall, I am heartburn—finches' wings. Stalks

being pulled from the incinerator. *After*

completing my poems I am

curious to review them in light

issues are published that count as two issues as indicated on
the issue's cover. Your first issue will arrive in 4-6 weeks. Offer
good in U.S. only.

EDCJ9KSJA1

BUSINESS REPLY MAIL
FIRST-CLASS MAIL   PERMIT NO. 349   HARLAN IA

POSTAGE WILL BE PAID BY ADDRESSEE

ELLE DÉCOR

PO BOX 6059

HARLAN, IA 51593-3559

ELLE DECOR

ONLY $1.⁵⁰
an issue!

of their intentions—the thirty

years they seek to embody. The painting,

the essay, grandfather with his medals. They were

well provided for. (See

"Benjamin," 1940.)

§

Le Moribond

after Jacques Brel

In the catacombs I am impatient.
    In this hall shuttling between

    one world and the next, from
nothing to being and back again,

I stand, restless, following the worm
    of thought to its blacked-out end:

    I study the bones before me,
observe fine cracks in the skulls,

hairline fractures, the pits of teeth
    gone missing. History compounds.

    The skulls are yellow, tar colored,
mangled with dust, tucked along

niches in the tunnels' run. I am not
    ready to be among them. And so,

    for now, I wait. Tonight I walk
the city's soft quays, watch mist

cloud over the Seine, people flicking
    cigarettes, striking guitars, strumming

    nickel strings—doing what
the French do. Empty bottles lounge

in the river. This far beneath ground
    one hardly hopes to escape. Femur,

tailbone, marrowless rib: tourists
pass photographing the dead, tombless

remnants unearthed by late priests.
　　Nightly their procession of cloth-

　　covered wagons emptied the city
cemeteries. A picture is a fine memento.

Bones tell us little. In this network
　　of interlaced tunnels six million

　　people lie buried. Many times
the walls collapsed, combining the bodies

of municipal workers with the ones
　　we find here. It adds them to the tomb.

　　The stacks of bodies are endless.
Now as I trace the path from one gray

lamp to another, the pattern of lights
　　between exits guides my walk

　　through the cold. Dark letters
urge me on, etched on a tableau of flat

stone: *Hault. Here is death's empire.*
　　Those who walk among them

　　no doubt return alive, though
occasionally, lovers lose their way,

spend a night or two among the dead.
　　My task is simple: leave the bones

interred. On the other side of these
dim-lit tunnels, sun attacks the nerves. Inveterate

monuments skulk from the square
    at Montparnasse. Their eyelids do not

    faze me. Death, whatever it is,
sleeps belowground. It doesn't mix

with the light. Fractures. Some of them died
    from only hairline fractures, enough

    to place silence in a grown man's teeth,
to plant his broken jaw beneath the dirt.

Spaghetti Western

In Georgetown, IN, the steel projector reels.
The desert stretches blankly before us, a red
plain constellated with rows of dry mesquite.

Stone wall, still screen, a single emptiness,
I suppose, throwing gray light over the tops
of parked cars. John Wayne surveying the valley

in a pair of seared chaps. Behind us, low hills
roll off. The highway, congested, winds
between them, an inflamed artery subjected

to cloud cover. Nothing avoids the firm
gaze of commerce: not the taut sky, the lake water
rippling beneath it. Not the fields of wild fennel,

their tiny yellow flowers scattering spore dust,
sycamores doing the same. "Tree sex," we say,
then nothing, cowboys rehearsing their pose.

Materia

I was interested in the violence of it all, the mariposa
          flowers wilting
in the heat. What my father said about

          sick Indians, flu
spread on the laundered habits of young nuns. "Indians,"
          that's what

he called them, shaving fence posts with a saw.
          Franciscans moved
among them, smudging their brows with crosses of ash.

          Incense trailed,
settled in the loose folds of their robes; someone
          at the altar trimmed

stems from fresh roses, poured wine into
          the decanter's mouth.
And here I am, meditative, fit for placid staring,

          lines of blue
across the page suggesting a vague idea of order.
          White embers

smolder. A glowworm wriggles from the pale
          leaf-loam. I never
pretended these woods were my own, the light

          a thin space to crawl into
when material failed me, mute speakers on the tent floor
          attesting to the actual world.

This is it, or something like it, untenable
        as anything. Once,
I wanted to grasp the flame's heat, to render it

        physically, or at least
· to put it into words. The soul, I'll take it by the river
        where the wind

stops; the mind, let it simmer at the fire's edge.
        Outside, clouds gather.
Rain beats the dirt road. Sun rays stream

        through breaks
between trees,
        gold motes dissembling.

Scarecrow

Clouds part and the sky appears as a ceiling's open vault,
this half-man stuffed and tethered to a post.

He's left for dead in dry wind, the mind's yearning for conceit.
I used to fall in love with words,—

Aspen, aspen aspen.
The dogwood's tortured trunk.

◆

Sun, sage, sycamore—
the sound of an ash tree falling in the woods.

A sheaf of red cloth soaked in rain
and knotted to a strand of barbed wire.

◆

Sometime in the space between this morning's prayer and afternoon
I saw a fox with her kits at the edge of the woods.

How soft they looked. And unafraid of the half-man
mounted in the corn. To them he might have seemed

beautiful, or passed for unobtrusive.
The fox led her kits to the stream for a drink of fresh water.

But then, the goats were at it again, bellying up
against the chicken wire and chewing on a scrap of torn cloth.

◆

Consider, for a moment, the cedar columns.
May we lay our dead there.

May it not require the body's return to the earth,
nor necessitate interaction with the soil.

＋

I wonder if the sun this year
will dry up all the fields.

Will the crows come then
if it dries up all the fields.

＋

I wonder *sun*, I wonder *seed*.

＋

It must have been about midnight when I saw a bat wheeling
in the air above the porch. It dipped in and out of light, catching

fruit flies in its mouth. I listened to the moth-lamp's hum
and began to whistle, wondering if the bat could see

the scarecrow standing sentinel in the dark.

＋

*—that the wrists, bound to wood planks, stretch out in the wind
like his.*

That's not the line I'm searching for.

＋

The crops stand in rows and I stand
to greet them, stare through the casement

at the congregating crows.

I am what *I* is not.
(The body, no, not bad.)

         ✦

No one's fooled by the half-man. No
thing. A black bird perches on a blade of straw

protruding from the scarecrow's shirt.

         ✦

An old man tilling the fields in March
dreams of salt and light.

Driving Arizona

Saguaro in headlights, we touch like foreign bodies.
Sedona recedes against the sky's aperture.
Roll the covers off, the coldness in Williams—
Aren't you afraid? I'm afraid, too.
Wanting to know you, thinking I do,
Thinking of the miles unfolding before us,
The highway beating through rows of golden cacti.

I want to remember things purely, to see them
As they are without the urge to order.
To take the pictures down, and say what hurts.
Say we're able to enjoy this more than we ever did.

Somewhere behind us, the mountains slope off.
Sunrise breaks over fields of whitened heather.
Let's only sit and listen. Only stare at the open earth
Without saying why. If approximations are the best
We can do—fine then, let's approximate.
Home is a question and we're drifting from it.

Catalogue Beginning with a Line by Plato

To the feasts of the good the good go unbidden.
Children's hands in snow. Houseboats on the lake,
a red and yellow bicycle. The scent of black cedar
severed in its prime.

When my father died the nickel
wire of my throat
       collapsed, snapped, twisted in air—

hung itself

       limply from the column of my neck.
(It's okay to play leapfrog in the yard.)

In the window sits a lampshade exhausted by light.
A man and woman riding home in the dark
warm the leather of their seats. A clownfaced wren
pecks bark from a pine, jams the acorns in a hole.

My mother slices plums on the counter,
removes the insides from their skin,
steeps lilac in a pot. The bubblegum
medicine she hauls from the drawer,
I take it from a spoon.

After Guatemala

1.

Slouching back to this cold coast, a calf-bone tucked
inside my hand, burned white in the dump heaps
of Mesoamerica.

2.

Sea-glass smoothed by the tide: licked clean on the ocean's floor
yet rude to the tang of sweet tamarind.

3.

Oranges—yes, we have those.
Avocado, we ravage it.

But nothing like the bloated, waxy leaves
from the South, bigger than my hand, and stippled
with blue dots.

4.

To ignore them

is to let a drape on the eyes,
to smoke taste from pecked fruit.

5.

Like a spent perfume, or the scent
of a wilted flower,
I first inhaled the thick air.

It broke upon my mouth as a cragged cough,
rust-flakes erupting from the lungs.

6.

Slowly, salivating, one learns.
And already these days taper to an end.

7.

Among the cast-off cargo and low dune sweeps
vestiges of jetsam roll in.
Light lessens; memory breeds warm blood.

And after sunscreen, after fire,
this is how it stands:
bleached bone, green sea, the cry of a common gull.

Delaware, I-95

Cattails at lakeside
constitute ecologies.
Telephone wires

dissect the sky, negate
the coast's rusted corridor.

Purple lupine
erupts in the median.
The sleeping child
on my leg dozes, becomes

aware, loses consciousness
again, her cheeks flanked
by marshlight, summer's hum,

the blue idola
of bug guts spattering the windshield
in the cold, mechanic
valence of the lamps

along the road, the round oaks
rapidly scuttering
into the sagged night, where thought's

low and turbid overflow
winds in.

At Assateague

The sun is a thin line of red
broadening over the bay.
It slices the horizon, strikes light
into a darkness poised
to disclose some secret the night
couldn't shake out of it.

Trout smokes over hot coals.
Wild ponies in the distance
charge along the strand, kick sand
up behind them, an inelegant cloud
that smears the dawn's gouache.

It's unbearable, this scene,
its sickening romance.

Still I want to hold it, to freeze
its sudden architecture
in the flotsam of the beach—
to suck the ichor from its rib.

It wouldn't sustain me, I know.
The gulls turning their circles
would grow dull.
I'd berate the sand flea's itch.
The gravitation of the tide's pull
would choke me with ennui.

Pear blossoms soon give way to pears,
I'll never stop eating them.

End

1.

A cloud steeps the gorge I drive beside.
　　The cars moving toward me are dull

bellies of yellow jackets washed in a sea
　　of bright foam. Time rushes—toward me,

and away. I hold the median, the rock
　　jutting from the river. In the fog

I hardly see it. Smoke settles around me
　　like a pocket of blue. I forget nothing;

nothing forgets. Carbon only remains.
　　The all of us pressed in a rock of mined coal.

Summer dissipates. The world
　　turns about. *Buckets*, the poet says, *of old*

light going home. I like the mystery of it.
　　I like to think the atoms of the stones

beneath the river are not the finite end,
　　that the south-departing mallards signal

something other than themselves.
　　Driving home, I feel the axel-hum,

liquid fossils exploding beneath the pedals
　　at my feet. Its gases fill the air. October

lasts no time at all. I pick my daughter
    up from school, rush against the clock.

The cells in her body divide. Mine
    decay. Already I feel a twitch in my eye.

Tendons, liver, heart. What's fixed
    is a constant going, the rapid ebb of states

of being rearranging themselves
    in the skin. The skin itself remains.

The wrinkles at my lip persist in their
    inordinate glory. The future is an idea

I've read about in any dozen online articles,
    as in this one about the dolphins

that swim two hundred miles up the Potomac
    avoiding pleasure cruisers. Only

the biologists know they're there.
    Knew. I guess the jig is up.

2.

Do we make our end or does it
    make us? My teeth are brittle

broken bones; the leaves yellow
    and fall. Outside there's a window

with music coming from it, the low
    tones of a recorded violinist.

The shells of half-dead beetles scatter
　　in the dung. Eternity's a farce.

The amber-trapped mosquito already
　　isn't there. I hold my breath, let

the wind envelop my skin until
　　the leaves decay. We'll be them.

Our cells salute the compost. Gnats
　　drift in sullen shafts of equinoctial light.

The end, we're moving toward it.
　　Toward it, and away. The days

are shorter now. The pumpkin
　　decomposing on the porch

volunteered its seeds in spring.
　　In the garden I watch a sunflower dip,

the birds pecking, gorging, dropping
　　empty shells onto the dirt. Their atoms

keep reshaping themselves. I step
　　to the window where the light

seeps between blinds, where music
　　dawns, and the little roar

of gathering swallows trickles in—
　　swallows moving toward us, drifting,

always toward us, lifting in the sky
　　and then away.

§

Kentucky, September

My grandfather stood outside smoking,
watching the migrant workers
bend over the bare furrow.
I was in the cross-barn stripping leaves
from green stalks, knowing God was cruel,
that he must be. Even on a map
South America looks like a sick heart.
I hung the leaves from tiered poles
and let them dry in the heat.

Once we found a she-goat dead,
her belly split, and blood trailing over
an arched rock. Something about
her innards spread across the ground
made me think of nakedness.
My grandfather took the carcass
in his arms and carried it to the driveway
where I said a short prayer.

Stripping finished for the night,
I sat next to my grandfather
on a wooden bench behind the barn,
hands beneath my legs, our backs
cocked against a bale of hay.
Bats erupted from the silo like buckshot.
Then I realized this wasn't my grandfather,
and these weren't my hands.
All of this was a pasture resembling heaven.
Heaven was a meadow in time.
The moon rose over the empty fields
wedging shadows together in the dirt.

Clock Elegy

Outside, the day collapses.
White moths crowd around the porch.

The hall clock runs like a whetting stone
turning in my stomach's pit.

With a spade my mom begins to dig,
shoveling dirt where the river's been.

I check the sleeves of my father's coat
for words he might have left.

Handbells, their tinny sound invades the yard.
Shad flies gather on the swollen lake.

Inside my mother smoothes the sheets
that stretch my father's bed.

By noon light pinholes through the clouds
but my eyes refuse to adjust.

Sirens. A warning sign.
I taste the cut in my mouth.

Years I've Slept Right Through

The field is steeped with the violence of horses.
Night descends blue hills
and I attempt to weigh distance,
as a calf tests its footing to the water hole.
On the front porch, my cat devours a hummingbird.
He beats the brilliant body with his tufted paws.
He breaks its wings,
swallows whole the intricate bone-house.

Inside, the pilot light is burning.
My sister's friend with the coal eyes is over.
Gradually, I crawl into bed, aching for more light.
In the dooryard
a young boy stoops to pluck
feather from feather until his hands are sore.
So prone to sadness, this thief—
I take my glasses off and lay them on the table.
The shadow of a tree rests inside my palm.

This spring I commemorate my father's death
by tacking deer-horns above the door.
My hammer strokes disperse
an assembly of hens,
waiting around for me to scatter their seed.

A mile away the river is abundant.
It breaks its sudden excess
on a limestone bridge.
A big-axled wagon tips into the water,
where white mud washes the coachman clean.
This is a custom he repeats every year,
coming and going until his wheels give out,
coming to wet his tongue.

Dawn chalks over the horizon
rendering the sky a storm-blotched red.
The outline of a cow appears on the hill
and then dissolves into the fog.
I follow her path with my ear,
listening as a bell sounds out the trail.
It is mine, this world
of bread and skin and stone.
Lay me in the field with all the fallen horses.

FIG. I

Botany

Chthonic

My light bulb is gone.
        It was dying anyways.
The room goes dark
        before I sleep. I lie,
eyes closed, listening,
        hoping the radio waves
cause only one type
        of sick. My bed's
not safe. The feathers
        in my pillow came
from a factory in Beijing.
        Their birds fly east
in the shape of a *V*.
        On the edge where
my mother sat reading
        a bright picture book
something has taken
        her place. My father's
mouth, which I lost
        years ago, speaks
from a jar on the shelf.
        I ask my mother
what she did with the light.
        She says it's
under the bed. I ask
        my father why
he can't hear. He tells
        me he's underground.

Poem Around Which Everything Is Structured

On his third night of dreams the boy turning in his bed
      hums about goodness and trees. He sees the berries
in his palm, which are the final berries of the season,

      so he squeezes them to watch their juice bleed through
the dim crevasses of his hand. Something's missing
      in this song and I don't know what it is. A shadow, maybe,

or a light between trees. Tonight, as the stars seep
      through his window and touch the dusty water he keeps
in a glass by his bed, the boy wonders what it would be

      to touch the body of another. I search his eyes
for mutual absence. And maybe as I map the freckles
      on his wrist, as the song crescendoes, as the night fades into

dull purples and blues—maybe the lights go out and I feel
      his breath on my hand. Or maybe that's wrong, too.
Maybe I become the delicate prison he attends to, the cold

      thread wending in and out his chest, the rapture he feels
when he dangles me from the wood post of his gallows.
      Suppose I wrote this song in another key entirely.

I could cast it in a way that doesn't care about touching
      and hips. The boy could carry a spade out into the yard
and drop it down into the soil, where the earth would dance

      around it and the stars shrink into the distance until they
disappear between hills. This is how I think, Love,
      about you. This is how I structure everything around me

that needs to be structured—the taste buds on your tongue,
        the salt of your wrist, the shape of your mouth as you
tell me every little thing you ever wanted me to know.

        I want to give him a name, that boy. I want to call that name
on nights when the ceiling hangs low above my bed,
        and the plaster cracks, and the sky pokes through the minute

slits between blinds. I want to feel his hands, not my hands,
        shivering in the wool sleeves of my coat, anything
but the same shaking of the leaves, the orchid dying bloom

        by bloom in the window while its naked stem bends
a single blossom toward the sun. It delights in a small
        cool mist. Let me speak plainly. Let me get to the dark

heart of the matter. The thing is, Love, that when I watch
        the squash buds wither, when the June sun makes them
shrivel into themselves, it's almost too much for me to bear.

        I see them—and that is all. I hear an emptiness in the wind,
and wrap my mind around it, and think of the king snake coiled
        in the grass. Soon he will be skin and bones. Already he is but

skin and bones. He rubs his head against a rock. The sun shines.
        Wood lice creep from the open dirt. Tonight, as the boy
turns in his bed, and wrestles with the prospect of his own

        approaching dusk, I bend myself above you, or below, whichever
way it is that you prefer. I breathe the clean grasses
        of your skin and unpack each assorted item you keep hidden

in a travel-sized box by your purse. And I, and the boy, sit
        blinking in the dark, staring off at the wall and the dead stars
beyond it throwing cold light through the black matter

of millennia. It rests inside his palm. It rests in mine. At times,
looking out at the bare sky, and watching those stars fizzle
    in the map of still time, I want to crawl up into its stillness,

and feel obsolete, distant from my father and the warm bodies
    I've touched, and watch through a tree so lovingly hollowed
their vague shapes flit between leaves. It's a problem

    in philosophy and form, each hand's different twenty-
seven little bones reaching out to hold the cloth
    draped upon the shoulders of another. Slowly,

those shapes come into focus, and the dawn light, which is
    not dead light, seeps into the room. In it, in the yard,
where the boy throws down his spade, and a mule-tailed deer

    licks dew from his palm, the apple trees shine, collard
stalks stiffen, the paper-white bark of an aspen
    quivers, Love, and the grasses shudder in unison, in wind.

FIG. 2

Roots | Tumble

Sonata

and the head sickens, and the liver sickens:

he will not wake up—my uncle with the tattooed

worm on his stomach, stretched out over years:

he lies symmetric on the operating table

holding his elbow, holding his skin under the lamp

that makes him feel small: my wrist brushes against

a numb sponge—that is his lip: my mother slides a finger

across the piano top, my legs stretched out as before:

as my mother's on the coffee table as we wait:

Chopin speaks, Bach speaks: we cry beside the piano:

and the bookshelves heavy with books:

and a closed room: and the doctor telling the story

of a gentle incision: my uncle among children

feeding breadcrumbs to geese: he notices the scar

on his chest: scars on the chests of the birds:

the mole on his granddaughter's cheek:

his eyes are gone and he's losing his hair:

he is naked and runs a hand over his belly and laughs:

and I am crying in the shower: my mother plays a scale:

and the story: he's humming himself to sleep

Erosion

I played with the sunlight splayed between grains, haloes
of ash around her sleeping eyes. Skeleton stalks moving
briefly in the yard. She told me about the bees, how in winter
they expel the crumpled bodies of their dead, dropping shells
one by one onto the dirt. Hive's center, the queen warms herself
on honey. I think of the artist who scooped them in her palm,
sealed them in bags, left them in the window. Wheat shocks,
summer dark. An hour lying in the grass. Emptiness itself cuts
along the bank. I wanted to make this vivid, so vivid. To say
a passerine flits in the wind. Pistil, stamen, pollen floods my nose,
powdering tent walls, the acne scars honeycombing her face.
Sea's rush, river's stop. Seepage from a well. Everyone believes
in one rapture or another. It is summer, I am thirsty. My canteen
is empty. There is not enough water. There was never enough water.

Heirloom (Wreck)

Hornets buzzing out from under branches.
        The sound of a circular saw.

The lake. A plane over the lake.
        Breath like a wave of cicadas.

From the porch I watch my mother's lips
        trying as I can to read her ghost talk.

In the morning, flood, the base of the hill.
        We gather at the river's edge.

Sandbags, a pile of them,
        stacked like rocks along the water.

I look to see where the river ends,
        I look to see my brother.

When the rain hits, still I'm not asleep.
        Low thunder on the open grass.

A slow bird beats its wings against my belly.
        I dream a burning house.

Other Adam

The stone moon descends to brush his shoulder clean, blood

Dewed around his wound. The newborn

Woman groans. His pony drinks from a bucket

Of stars. She shrinks to his side to replace

     A stolen rib. Startled, her hips flit. Birds in her throat,

In his. Hand to his side, his veins the shade of rivers—

Danube, Thames, Tigris, and Euphrates.

Ohio or Mississippi. In his dream a nomad smacks a tambourine

And drops a lantern at his feet. Dancers, their skirts

Flower as they spin. The woman puts her fingers in

His side, feels around until she finds the

          Heart, a cello

Pulsing at his center. She lifts it, trying to discern

What makes his body move.

             He mutters

In his sleep. Somewhere in the grass a cobra's

Fanning its neck. The liquid pearled on his thigh shines like milk

Pooled in a thicket of reeds. The woman curls next

To him on the ground and in her sleep she sees

      The ocean, orange trees, a path through

The markets of Jaffa where she wanders aimlessly until

Her face morphs into a limp pear. She doesn't

Know that she is naked. Rain collects in

          The small of her back.

FIG. 3

Colonialisme

Beneath the Trees at Ellingsworth

I wake in an orchard chaotic
                          with apple blossoms.
                Kentucky, I know it from the smell.

Field where my dog spun circles
                                    in blue light
        collapsed
                bleeding from the mouth.

We piled limestone in the yard to keep the coyotes out.
                Covered the grave
                          and marked it with a wooden cross.

My brother knots his shirt on sheep wire
                          scores his stomach on the rusted barbs.

His name cuts my lung like split glass—
                frost in the hollow of a throat
        I can't remember.

The heart's heat begins to slow.
                          I climb apple tree
        after apple tree.

§

Forget the Song

I specified said light on the ladybugs, their dead shells accumulating on the

windowsill. What is better—exodus or testament. What comes first, the

thought or the word, the word or desire—ash trees wilting by the creek.

In the beginning, everything is whole. My daughter cuts her first tooth.

Then sound, its jarring simplicity—I catch her mouthing for words. She

sighs, she fidgets. She coos in the dark, in the room where she never sleeps.

—

Rain spatters the window.

I try to understand fiber

optic cable—light slowed to the pace

of material transfer, the hair

thin glass for medical imaging.

I look toward the sun—light

travels through air. It fills

the blood in my hand. Days

grow short, the warped

oak stands, whorl

of whorls, the wood

equivalent of an ear. Daughter,

danger—everything is danger.

The marble dropped

on the floor. The instability

of a bookcase in the most non-

metaphysical terms. I spend

the morning thinking

about sound, how it registers

muffled from the corner

opposite its origin,

thus the introduction

of error, the flaw

in the perceiving tool.

—

We think, we sense, we *are—life opens it opens it is / breaking.*

Open, the serviceberry bud shoots its seed. Light knives

the leaves, their cells. Where, I think, are the monarchs—orange

flames ablaze. It's been one of those weeks. Working

the garden this morning, I unearthed a pale bug, groped

for a name—"white grubworm." I watched it wriggle on the surface

until I shaped the dirt mounds, buried it somewhere in the heap.

—

A black wick curled in the candle's flame,

        braided cotton converting to ember.

It furls into itself. Today I moved a box

turtle from the road. This was after

        a brief rain. The concrete there is warm.

He settled in the grass. Later, beer,

        the redbud blossoms. The earth beneath

the blueberry plants is only slightly acidic.

Notes

"The Milk Hours" takes its title from Carolyn Forché's "Blue Hour," to which it owes a debt.

The italicized text in section two of "History (n.)" is excerpted from G. W. F. Hegel's *Lectures on the Philosophy of History*. Those in lines one through three of section three come from Arthur Schopenhauer's *The World as Will and Representation*; seven and eight of section three from Friedrich Nietzsche's *On the Genealogy of Morality*; that in section four from Haruki Murakami's *The Wind-Up Bird Chronicle*. Section five is excerpted in its entirety from Plato's *Phaedo*. The italicized text in line two, section six, is excerpted from Anne Carson's *Nox*, lines three and four from *The Wind-Up Bird Chronicle*.

"Metamorphoses" borrows a line, slightly altered, from Henri Cole's "Beach Walk," with which it is otherwise in conversation.

Line one of "April, Andromeda" borrows from Dan Beachy-Quick's *This Nest, Swift Passerine*. *The Book of Fixed Stars* is an Arabic astronomical text written around 964 by the Persian astronomer Abd al-Rahman al-Sufi; the US Library of Congress houses a fifteenth-century manuscript of the text. The italicized language in section three is excerpted and lineated from Henry David Thoreau's *Walden*. That in section six is excerpted and lineated from Ralph Waldo Emerson's essay "Memory." The italicized text in sections seven and nine is excerpted and deliberately corrupted from John Keats's "If By Dull Rhymes Our English Must Be Chain'd." That in section ten is excerpted from Herman Melville's *Moby-Dick*.

"Poem for the Nation, 2016" begins on a line from Ada Limón's "A New National Anthem."

The title of "Klee's Painting" refers to Paul Klee's *Angelus Novus*. The first instance of italics, in section one, comes from Virginia Woolf's *Mrs. Dalloway*. Those in section two are excerpted, and slightly altered, from Walt Whitman's essay "A Backward Glace O'er Travel'd Roads." The italicized lines in section three are excerpted variously from the Whitman essay and Gerard Manley Hopkins's "Pied Beauty."

"Erosion" echoes a line from Brandon Kreitler's "Valley as a Negative." The poem is for Carrie Burr, who knows these bees too well.

The italicized text in section three of "Forget the Song" is excerpted and shaped from W. S. Merwin's "The Birds on the Morning of Going," which appears in *The Carrier of Ladders*.

Figs. 1-3 were collaged from images sourced on the British Library's Flickr Commons page. Many thanks to the curators for making this resource available for public disruption.

Acknowledgments

Thank you to the editors of the following publications in which this work first appeared, sometimes in an earlier version:

Adroit Journal: "Fig. 1" (as "Botany")
Boston Review: "Metamorphoses"
California Journal of Poetics: "Forget the Song"
Columbia Poetry Review: "Beneath the Trees at Ellingsworth"
Copper Nickel: "Scarecrow"
DIAGRAM: "Kentucky, September"
Harpur Palate: "Years I've Slept Right Through"
Kenyon Review: "History (n.)"
Louisville Review: "The Milk Hours"
Massachusetts Review: "Other Adam"
Meridian: "Poem Around Which Everything Is Structured"
Missouri Review: "At Assateague," "End," and "Le Moribond"
New Madrid: "Driving Arizona"
Palimpsest: Yale Graduate Literary & Arts Magazine: "Materia" and "Spaghetti Western"
Phantom: "Sonata"
Poetry Northwest: "Poem for the Nation, 2016"
Portland Review: "After Guatemala"
Quarterly West: "Fig. 2" and "Fig. 3" (as "Roots | Tumble" and "Colonialisme," respectively)
Redivider: "Clock Elegy"
Tinderbox Poetry Journal: "Erosion"
Tupelo Quarterly: "April, Andromeda"
Vinyl: "Heirloom (Wreck)"
West Branch: "Klee's Painting"
Western Humanities Review: "Catalogue Beginning with a Line by Plato"

Thank you to Natasha Trethewey for selecting "History (n.)" to appear in *Best American Poetry 2017*, to Brenda Shaughnessy for choosing "Chthonic" for *Best New Poets 2013*, and to Mary Szybist, who included my "Poem Around Which Everything Is Structured" in *Best New Poets*

2016. Thanks, too, to Kevin Prufer, who selected my work for Columbia University's Academy of American Poets Prize and to an anonymous reader at Georgetown University for granting me the Ora Mary Pelham Poetry Prize, also from the Academy of American Poets. "The Milk Hours" appeared on Poets.org as part of this award. "Spaghetti Western" was featured as Split This Rock's Poem of the Week in February 2018 and is archived online at *The Quarry: A Social Justice Poetry Database*. Thanks to Sarah Browning—for this, and so much more.

Some of these poems appeared in *Chthonic*, a chapbook published by CutBank Books in 2015. Thanks to Allison Linville and the CutBank team for putting it into the world. Others appeared in a limited edition art book, *The Field Is a Good Place to Die*, with photographs by Carrie Marie Burr, organized for a multimedia exhibition at PYRO Gallery in Louisville, Kentucky. Thank you to Carrie for collaborating with me and to Jeffrey Skinner for inviting me to participate.

Showers of gratitude to my teachers: Carolyn Forché read this manuscript in full and offered shape to its natural chaos. Timothy Donnelly taught me to interrogate what, at first glance, I resist. For that, I am grateful. Lucie Brock-Broido, who unfortunately did not live to see this book to fruition, unleashed the feral cat inside of me. Eamon Grennan and Mark Strand read and responded to very early versions of this book, when it was still an MFA thesis. Nathan K. Hensley is an intellectual giant. His comments on my scholarship informed my approach to creativity: they are, to my mind, two sides of the same coin. Frederick Smock, my first mentor, showed me how to write with clarity and specificity, and with an eye for the natural world. No one deserves more thanks than him.

The following people supported me in myriad ways, either by critiquing individual poems, writing on my behalf, nurturing my thought in relation to poetics, or by offering encouragement when at crucial moments I doubted this work or its relevance: Corey Waite Arnold, E.C. Belli, Dan Beachy-Quick, Jennifer Chang, Kyle and Marie Coma-Thompson, Eduardo C. Corral, Jay Deshpande, Julia Guez, Alen Hamza, Dave Harrity, Eric Helms, Sean Patrick Hill, Jeff Hipsher, John Fenlon Hogan, Rebecca Gayle Howell, Justin Keenan, Ada Limón, Sarah Manguso,

Brandon Menke, Bellamy Mitchell, Jewel Pereyra, Nathaniel Caleb Perry, Joy Priest, Danniel Schoonebeek, Krystal Anali Vasquez, Ken L. Walker, and so many others. This book wouldn't have existed without you.

Indescribable thanks to Henri Cole for selecting the book, for graciously offering his thoughtful suggestions, and for believing in the possibilities these poems attempt to unfold.

Thanks to everyone at Milkweed for making it real: to Daniel Slager, Joey McGarvey, Abby Travis, Jordan Bascom, and the entire team. You are magic.

This book wouldn't be possible without the generous support of Ariella Ritvo-Slifka and the Alan B. Slifka Foundation. I never met Max, but we had the Columbia community in common, and it's an honor to be able to memorialize him in this small way. Thank you.

And finally, but most importantly, gratitude unending to my loving and in-credibly supportive family: to Clementine, Mom, Mike, Shelby, Joe, Kimi Jo, and the late Alvy and Tako. And to Sarah, my best and most arduous critic, especially when we disagree: this book is better for your insights, argumentation, and your love. Each of you made these poems, more than you know.

~

This book is for my father, John E. James, whose absence became the *via negativa* through which these poems were born.

Gina Collecchia

John James was born in California and raised in Kentucky. He is the author of *Chthonic*, winner of the 2014 CutBank Chapbook Prize, and his poems appear in *Boston Review, Kenyon Review, Gulf Coast, Poetry Northwest, Best American Poetry 2017*, and elsewhere. Also a visual artist, his collages have been published in *Quarterly West* and *Adroit Journal*. He lives in the San Francisco Bay Area, where he is pursuing a PhD in English at the University of California, Berkeley.

The second award of the

MAX RITVO POETRY PRIZE

is presented to

JOHN JAMES

by

MILKWEED EDITIONS

and

THE ALAN B. SLIFKA FOUNDATION

Designed to honor the legacy of one of the most original
poets to debut in recent years—and to reward outstanding
poets for years to come—the Max Ritvo Poetry Prize
awards $10,000 and publication by Milkweed Editions to
the author of a debut collection of poems. The 2018 Max
Ritvo Poetry Prize was judged by Henri Cole.

Milkweed Editions thanks the Alan B. Slifka Foundation
and its president, Riva Ariella Ritvo-Slifka, for supporting
the Max Ritvo Poetry Prize.

milkweed
editions

Founded as a nonprofit organization in 1980, Milkweed Editions is an independent publisher. Our mission is to identify, nurture and publish transformative literature, and build an engaged community around it.

milkweed.org

Interior design by Mary Austin Speaker
Typeset in Adobe Jenson Pro

Adobe Jenson was designed by Robert Slimbach for Adobe
and released in 1996. Slimbach based Jenson's roman styles
on a text face cut by fifteenth-century type designer Nicolas Jenson,
and its italics are based on type created by Ludovico Vicentino
degli Arrighi, a late fifteenth-century papal scribe
and type designer.